SOLID
TRUTHS &
TESTIMONIALS:
VOLUME 2
DEAR GOD

Janetta Lynne Jones

Printed by: Amazon.com for:

Janetta Lynne Jones
Independent Publisher
Tallahassee, Florida

ISBN: 9798811858866
LCCN: 2022905958

Cover designer: Kenya Wolf

Intro

God, You said I could come as I am, and I came hurt, confused, lost, beaten down, drained, tired, broken, and the list could go on and on. But You didn't specify the attire or the package, so I just showed up with open arms hoping for acceptance, peace of mind, and hope that You could make me whole and feel brand new in the spiritual world. I am out of ammunition on earth, and Satan and his demons need to be rebuked and cast down back to hell. I come before You humble and in prayer because the people need to understand that You are a wonderful supernatural miraculous being worthy of fellowship; one who endures solid friendships and sincere conversations, and that's why I have been looking for You.

My eyes were finally opened up, and my heart stopped hesitating and started processing the truth about this battle of life. Only I can control my actions and not the actions of people around me. I can only follow the instructions going where You, not the wolves in sheep's clothing, have ordered my steps to lead. (It's Your will, not my will, God).

I have realized that You were my blanket all this time, and You were the peace that has overcome me in my times of need and throughout my whole life. You are my hero! If the people, who are my true critics, pay attention to the cover and back of this book and the first one I wrote, they will see that the flames are out on the scroll and my hand is reaching up for You. I have come in peace.

Your ears are so powerful that no prayer goes unheard or unanswered, and anything that was not received in my requests was never asked for or desired. I don't worry about what man says because I know all things are possible with You. Even though I admit I am not always consistent in prayer, I am always aligned with You as I go on with my daily queen duties.

I decided to put some of my solid private truths and experiences into a volume to share our love for each other with the world. (We all have individual and unique relationships).

Facing adversity is my strong suit. I am at my best when my back is against the wall, anxiously expecting You to intervene in Your perfect timing. I titled this book *Dear God* because I want the people to know that it is okay to vent and be open about their trials, tribulations, and testimonials. You know my heart better than anybody on this planet. I don't care what the naysayers, the Christians, or any religion says about my dialogue when it comes to You.

I am who I am, God, and I am not changing for this world; I'm only changing for You. And I will not let these so-called Christians or followers tell me how to conduct myself when it comes to Your love for me either because I think that some of them have forgotten that You found them or they found You in a dark lonely place. (They were lost and broken, too).

You told me that I could come as I am, and I came unafraid, wanting the world to read about my experiences and feel my soul's rawness and authenticity when it comes to us. It is also a display that these Kings and Queens can come as they are without feeling judged or critiqued because of what society says or thinks about how the Almighty should be approached, when His arms are always open and ready to embrace.

Dedication

To my daddy: Thank you for loving me continuously and unconditionally while I still struggle to love myself.

Opening Prayer

Dear God,

I heard a song on the radio today. It broke me down into tears. I was trying to figure out how I wanted to express my feeling of neediness for the love of You, God, and the urgency to feel comfortable in my skin and Your presence. Fantasia has this song on her album, *Sketchbook*, called "Looking for You" (featuring Mama Diane) that spoke to my soul. My heart stood still and listened while trying to get myself together. It's one of the few times in my life I was left feeling speechless because she sang what I didn't have the courage to admit out loud—I am still broken.

I've been looking for You, God, and I must say what a wonderful friend I have in You, especially when I acknowledge You and not get in the way of Your will for my life. This has been one heck of a season of speaking my truth, learning lessons of love, lost friendships, and the acceptance of my loneliness. You have guided me and redirected me with Your promises, and I have had to take some of my advice from *Solid Truths and Testimonials: Volume 1*. I've been looking for You.

God, You have always allowed me to speak my truth. I always knew when push came to shove, without any hesitation, You would love me, carry me, protect me, and see me through life's tribulations because this world has failed me, and You were all I had to depend on. Your love continuously uplifted me and inspired me to hold on tight to my guardian angel of purpose. That's why I am who I am today. I've been looking for You.

Fantasia named everything in her song: hope, strength, love, peace, and most of all—a friend, which is what I am in desperate need of. It seems like friendships are not trustworthy anymore, and love in relationships is not solid anymore. The people in and not of this world don't seem to have the intentions of respecting my boundaries, the foundation of my truth, recognizing my growth, and putting respect on my name because I am a legacy of prosperity. I am waiting for a supernatural breakthrough from You. I can't keep on feeling uncertainty or whether I am coming or going when the seasons change. I am looking for You.

Do You see my growth, God, or am I growing in Your eyes? Life is so unpredictable that sometimes I feel all four seasons in twenty-four hours. The book of Revelations is making itself clear every time I turn on the TV and see what's happening all over the world. I am looking for You.

I figure if I write down my thoughts, God, then maybe You can help me put out the flames to my scroll. Then some of my solid truths that are paralyzing my growth to be the mother I need to be for my daughter and the woman I need to be for myself will inspire other kings and queens on the journey to the discovery of self-healing and self-love. I'm glad I found You. Amen.

Table of Contents

DEAR GOD, IT'S ME, JANETTA

Untitled #40

Dear Birth Father,

I do not even know where to begin. But at 2:40 p.m. on Wednesday, May 26, 2021, I feel that this is a good start to relay all my feeling and emotions about an unknown person that has been absent from my life for forty-one years. I did not come to make any accusations; I do not know all the facts. I come in peace, just wanting to know the truth if you are willing to tell it. So, could you please allow me a few minutes of your time? My heart is open, and I am willing to listen, knowing that every story has two sides. Before I point the finger or have my gut stir up any emotions being positive or negative, I will listen, process, and then come to my conclusion after everything is taken in and you have said your piece.

I honestly do not know why you did not step up to the plate if my biological mother did not want me. And if that was the case, I guess the real question is, did you even know about me, or have you been living your life in the dark not knowing that you have a baby girl who has been living in this big old world without you? I cannot really complain about negligence. God blessed me with a great man whom I call daddy. But because of our struggles, I often wonder if you would have been anything better, or am I just better off not knowing who you are?

I was wondering if I was a mistake? Was I carelessly conceived because of not wanting to use any protection? Was I meant to be thrown out in a napkin, a stain on somebody's couch, or washed away into misery in somebody's washing machine? They say accidents do happen. But since I made it through the nine-month baking

11

stage, I am alive and well with purpose. Look at how God showed out when He brought me into existence. I have survived people, things, and situations that were supposed to break me, kill me, and even numb me. But instead of folding, I rose to the occasion. Sometimes it took months and years to get my feet planted on solid ground.

Biological father, I need to know who you are and where you went because your blood is me. I need to know what generational curses need to be broken, or have I succeeded them already? I need to know what kind of man you are. I am not going to allow the past to dictate how I am feeling about whatever decisions you have made. I have made some decisions, too, and everybody needs to be healed and forgiven because of our immaturity.

Are you open-minded to witnessing a live birth from a grown woman trying to get to the seed of where I came from? Biological father, my truth has been solidified. I have nothing but love for you. I forgive all the hurt that not knowing you has caused me because the man in my life is tough but sufficient. My daddy has loved me like no other. He has stood by my side despite how aggravated and irrelevant he made me feel at times.

I love this man with all my heart, and I would not trade him for the world.

Not even for you.

Untitled #41

Dear God,

There were a lot of things left unsaid and a lot of emotions I should have expressed to my brother while he was here. But the way I remember growing up, certain phrases like *I love you* were rarely heard. I did not understand how deep he and I were connected until the day I saw him on his back being viewed in the casket. I was my brother's keeper. Some might disagree, but they can kiss my backside. I was the watchdog who got help and called for my dad, Mrs. Jones, or both whenever he was in a crisis. I was terrified from seeing him in a state that my adrenaline wouldn't allow me to remain calm enough to help him. I was scared. Like a coward, I stood and watched him feeling helpless. My regret is that I should have done more.

I was protective of my brother when circumstances allowed, and I always kept watch because I was always concerned for his safety. There were a lot of secrets and regrets of his that I knew of. I nosily stumbled across some notes stating his hopes and dreams that I respectfully will not speak on because it is a sensitive issue. That is a button that I am not willing to press just to get my point of truth across. I was thirsty to find out indirectly what made him happy besides reading, cooking, coffee, and technology.

My brother knew he was going to die, and I am going to solidify that truth. I witnessed this man handle critical health issues with so much grace that I used to just stare at him and wish we could trade places. I tip my crown to him because not everybody can handle the cards that life deals them like he did. I remember when he moved back home. I noticed he looked different from when he'd left to live his life unapologetically, unafraid, and independent. I noticed he moved differently than before. He was so routine until I felt that nobody but me recognized he was making his peace while preparing for his transition.

I was in disbelief when I peeked inside the room and was forced to face the reality that I was paying my final respects and saying goodbye, but only for now. Reality forced me to realize that he was now a bittersweet memory. His death moved me in a way that I could not fully grieve. Even though I kissed his cold forehead, I was still in denial. I was angry because he was a good person. I could not understand. Out of the millions of people in this world, why him? I felt guilty because he was so good and empathized with my thirst for knowledge. He always took the time to help me and made sure I understood, and I know he loved me despite the fact that I felt misunderstood.

I loved my brother dearly. As I look back at our relationship, I wish I had said it more. I wish I had been more compassionate to his will to live. The dark angel of sickness beat him down unmercifully. Watching him suffer hurt me inside and out because there was nothing I could do to save him but assist my parents with whatever was needed to bring him comfort.

The one thing I will say is that individuals have to enjoy the ones around them who are close because this life is the one thing that is not guaranteed. When God calls us home, there is not a vaccination, a cure, or a praying oil that can be blessed across the forehead to keep us from crossing over to the other side.

I knew my brother was tired, and I knew he was ready. I regret I took our time for granted, and I wish I could go back and use it wisely by listening, understanding, and being more comforting. Amen.

Untitled #42

Dear God,

Please ask people to give me my flowers while I am here on top of the soil, and do not wait until I am gone. What matters to me is how I am loved. Please have them acknowledge the woman I have become because the defiant, selfless, young brat has been put to rest. And for information purposes, she no longer exists. So they can stop searching because they will not find her.

May the old me rest in peace and the new me be filled with much knowledge, wisdom, and experience, carry on, and live forever in peace, prosperity, and harmony. I want to make a toast to new beginnings, living with purpose while moving onward, and letting the past be just what it is—the past! Cheers.

Life is unscripted and unpredictable. And as myself, not an actor, I must play my role and deliver whatever emotions are presented in the unknown second, minute, and hour of the day as genuine and raw. The fake and the emotionless will get booed, and the one nonnegotiable thing is the last breath before transition. So today, I am leaving my heart on the stage with unrehearsed lines, standing with the spotlight beaming over me with my crown demanding respect, recognition, and authority over my life. It is my time to shine.

Give me my flowers because I have loved, and I have loved hard, not wanting anything but the love returned. I have carried my cross through adversity by taking and sucking up the pain of affliction from hardships of life's ups and downs while somehow managing to pick myself back up after hitting the ground face first. Worldly desires have contaminated me; even antibiotics cannot get rid of the infections transferred to me from broken souls.

Every day I struggle to want to live for you, God. Still, I fall short because of life's disappointments by limiting what I feel is impossible when everything about You is possible and unlimited. Even if someone cannot give me a dozen roses, at least give me a rose to validate my growth of being strong, especially when it appears that I am weak. I need to know that somebody cares. I need to know that somebody can identify with my struggle and the humility of God's grace.

Untitled #43

Dear God,

As much as I want to say this to my daddy's face while looking him dead in his eyes, I cannot because You will not like my gut-wrenching truth. However, I will say what I need to get off my chest on paper because my dad and I might never speak again. (Who knows, I am willing to take that chance). I would rather him reread my words than exchange explanations back and forth. I am just taking a few minutes out of my time to gather my thoughts and trying to figure out how to still be respectful to him and in control.

It is hard to come in peace with my non biological dad considering he has destroyed my inner peace, and I can no longer be silent or cordial. I must stand my ground; I must be heard. I am ready to delete reruns of the past that keep replaying in my head. (He probably has forgotten). When I was little, I did not know how to defend myself when he was slapping me around like I was a piece of trash. I think that my dad was a coward for swinging his fists at me to this day. If he only knew the mental and emotional damage he has caused me, maybe he would apologize. (I am not going to hold my breath on this one).

I have a child now; I have to catch myself. When I am angry, I try to mimic his foolishness, which scares me. My Tory does not deserve to be treated as if she is nobody, and even as a child, she deserves to be respected.

All I could do was cradle into a fetal position to protect whatever sense I had left because his behind could sure hit hard. (Defense

18

mechanism). It did not matter how mad I made him or how bad his day was, he was supposed to be my protector. But instead, I was the punching bag. (Worthless). Mrs. Jones or nobody in the house came to my defense, especially when they knew he was dead wrong. (Betrayed). A deaf ear turned to my screams and cries. Nobody had my back, and I felt like nobody gave a flip.

It is hard to hate him because of the love, patience, and consistency he has been in my life. It all balances out, and the good outweighs the bad. No matter how hard I try to tip the scale, my dad's love always wins.

My daddy taught me how to ride a bicycle. We had the whole neighborhood watching, and I felt proud. I remember him picking me up, dusting me off, and coaching me on how to stay focused and petal forward, but I kept my eyes on him. He taught me how to tell time. He kept me up all night until I grasped the concept. I was so mad with him, but I learned. I can go on and on about everything he has done and been in my life, but that is a book I am saving for a later date. Right now, I need healing.

I am strong because of my daddy. I am one hell of a woman, daughter, and fighter. I would not know how to give up on life or myself if instructed. I succeeded in everything he thought I could not do or expected me to do. I spent my life trying to live a dream for my daddy to get the recognition that my brother and sister received but failed every time.

I wasted years wrestling with the outside world. He failed me because the validation, love, and comfort I needed were silenced while struggling to identify where I fit in. I have heard his cries and seen his tears, so respecting him is necessary. He has been supportive and the superman I did not deserve. I love you, Dad.

In conclusion, daddy, you built me up to be strong, independent, and fierce but had one hell of a way of tearing me down. I will come in peace to agree to disagree. However, no matter how angry I am or get, the obstacles I put you through and took the family through were uncalled for. As an adult, I have come to realize that you have feelings, too. Amen.

Untitled #44

Dear God,

Today, I did the impossible. In a million years, I never thought I would envision or replay this scenario in my head about my father, but I have over a thousand times. It makes me sad and sick to my stomach that this will be my reality one of these days. While he is existing, I am scrambling my brain, trying to figure out coping mechanisms by understanding the stages of grief: denial, anger, bargaining, depression, and acceptance. I don't want him to die, but death is a fact; it is a devastating lifelong process I don't have the courage to face. I can't imagine my life without him, so I won't. It's mandatory that I live my life to the fullest and give him his flowers while he is still here.

I am trying to make myself as present as possible by observing wisdom and recognizing the growth of an accomplished man who will live on in the flesh and as a burning star in the universe for eternity, one day. Just imagine looking up in the sky seeing my daddy shining over me.

The love I have for him is unimaginable, and the love he is showing me is overwhelming on all levels. This man has loved me and still is giving me life when I have tried to assassinate his character and embarrass him with my wicked ways of being wet behind the ears in worldly behavior. The devil does not discriminate on race, age, or gender to seek, kill, or destroy. I have allowed him to use me on numerous occasions to break a man that was brought into my life to heal and protect me, talking about being ungrateful.

God, You said in Your first commandant that I may not love anyone or anything more than I love You, but how is that possible? This man has physically wiped my tears for comfort and created some by scolding my bad behavior while correcting me and allowing me to make mistakes. He is always giving me room for growth. I will never be him, but my dream is to be reserved, mild-tempered, in control, disciplined, and as accomplished as my earthly father one of these days.

God, what if I flip the script and die before him and the thoughts, concerns, and fears I have placed on myself become his concerns or reality? Will my dad be able to live without me? What memory of me will he hold on to? Sometimes, it feels like I have created more bad ones than good ones. God, You said in Matthew 10:37, "Anyone who loves their father or mother more than me is not worthy of me." Then you go on to say in verse 39, "Whoever does not take up their cross and follow me is not worthy of me." But really, God?

Every day I wake up and step out on faith, believing in a higher power I cannot see but feel deep in my heart it exists. I feel it guiding and protecting me from sitting high and looking low. Every day I am carrying my cross, but I may not be as righteous as some or as quick to forgive as most; but for the most part, I try to treat people as I want to be treated.

·I am constantly trying to stay optimistic, especially by smiling and fake grinning to individuals who keep doubting my abilities and are on the sideline, waiting to see me fail. My father has dealt with the highs and lows of my identity crisis. Therefore, it's hard to love You more. But because Your forgiveness and unconditional love are just as sufficient as his, I guess I have no choice because I was Yours first—before he became mine.

Living in this world without him will be the hardest thing I will ever have to do. So instead of preparing and bracing for the impossible thought, let me go first, God. I saw and remembered the tears my dad cried for my brother when he died, and I would rather it be his love loss than mine. Amen.

Untitled #45

Dear God,

Every day when I wake up to face the unpredictable world and wash my face while reciting my daily affirmations: *Queen, you are beautiful. Queen, you are a difference-maker. Queen, I dare you to go out into the world to prosper because you know your capabilities. You are that woman who always shows up and does what the naysayers say you cannot do, which is rise to the occasion.* Yes, I have the audacity!

Sometimes, I got to speak life into my spirit. If I wait for somebody else to do it, I will break down and surely die. I have a purpose; I have a voice I choose to use in this final destination. I have to be my cheerleader and quarterback, and I got to lead and motivate my movement. Depending on a hype man might be a two-faced digger digging my grave to self-destruct, forgetting to dig his own. Powerful!

I feel like nobody wants to see me win, but I am solidifying my truth. The circle is getting semi, and I feel like I have been left all alone. Karma is real, and the anointing I have on my life will not allow any casualties or weapons to prosper. (Talking about being covered with the blood of Jesus).

I speak my truth, and my goal is to continue living in it and speaking from the blood that flows through my four chambers, my heart. I will be bold under the sun no matter how hot, uncomfortable, human, and sticky the conditions may become. I trust that the Lord will send gestures like a cool breeze or just enough wind so that my determination will be kept and my eyes focused on the prize.

Every day when I wake up to face the unknown and unpredictable world, I wash my face while reciting my daily affirmations: *Queen, you are beautiful. Queen, you are a difference-maker. Queen, I dare you to go out into the world to prosper because you know your capabilities. You are that woman who always shows up and does what the naysayers say you cannot do, which is rise to the occasion.* Yes, I have the audacity!

I have to win before I leave this earth, and my destiny will be fulfilled. God has put something on my heart that will live on, and my destiny will recycle itself in history as one of the best that ever lived. Amen.

Untitled #46

Dear God,

Today, I woke up focused and more determined to be consistently positive about my future and keep my faith and trust in You no matter my circumstances. I am no longer making excuses and dragging my feet through the mud, waiting for a supernatural power to miraculously bring me immediate success when I know I have to speak firmly while moving mountains, become stronger while wrestling with harsh winds, stay poised while withstanding Sahara heat desert temperatures and tolerating unbearable humidity to rightfully claim my throne to be crowned as a queen.

I am just not anybody, God; I am a revolutionary black woman who has profoundly altered her life when the odds were against me. I turned the impossible to possible, and all the things the naysayers thought I couldn't do, I did. I am an immensely talented writer who is turning pain into pleasure by publishing and creating a legacy, succeeding at speaking my truth, and rising to face all oppressors who have shunned me and left me for dead, so the pigeons and crows could pick me and leave me stinking in the sun. I am not dead yet; the heart is still pumping, and the blood is still flowing. I refuse to die.

I will not give up. My daughter is watching. So every move I make must be my best one, not allowing room for mistakes. I refuse to die when there is so much purpose and unspoken thoughts I need to get out on paper and into the world when people refuse to hear my voice. The adrenaline is at an all-time high. With that being said, failure is not an option for this queen. I will rise to the occasion!

God, You said in Matthew 6:33-34, "But seek first His kingdom and His righteousness, and all these things will be given to you as well. Therefore, do not worry about tomorrow, for tomorrow will worry about itself. Each day has enough troubles of its own."

I am putting my heart in this Untitled because I have nowhere else to put this muscle and the safest place I know is in Your hands because man has failed me, friends have failed me, and so has my family. I am guilty of being hypocritical at times and doubting my faith concerning the promises You have committed to me because of my insecurities. But You said I could have all my heart desires, and I get frustrated when things are not going my way.

Psalm 37:4 states, "Take delight in the Lord, and He will give you the desires of your heart. He will make your righteous reward shine like the dawn, your vindication like the noonday sun." I am working towards that by speaking my truth, anxiously preparing for my rewards.

God, I lied in the beginning when I said I woke up determined, but I wasn't kidding about the being consistent part. Today was a struggle, and I woke up worrying about money, resources, success, and the legacy I want to leave behind for my daughter. Amen.

Untitled #47

Dear God,

You said in Romans 12:17-19, "Do not repay anyone evil for evil. Be careful to do what is right in the eyes of everyone. If it is possible, as far as it depends on you, live at peace with everyone. Do not take revenge, my dear friends, but leave room for God's wrath, for it is written: It is mine to avenge; I will repay," says the Lord." Now listen here, God, because this word from Your mouth is a tough pill to swallow. I have choked and gasped a couple of times because this Scripture alone kills my pride. I have often disobeyed it, especially when I have felt like seeking revenge and willingly accepting whatever repercussions might fall behind my actions. I have held vengeance strongly in my heart for others who have wronged me, but I'm not going to speak on it on the record just in case Karma decides she wants to show her face. So with that being said, I'm in a good place right now. I come in peace.

God, knowing that You are perfect is enough and sufficient. Knowing that there is nobody like You is mind-blowing, and I will only answer to You.

I'm all about speaking my truth. I can admit that I have not always been the best friend, daughter, companion, or any other word that You would associate with another individual. I can also say, without anyone trying to discredit my position by trying to expose me or embarrass me, that I have thought about taking vengeance on plenty of occasions, and I have. You said I could repent. Luke 17:3-4, "If your brother or sister sins against you, rebuke them; and if they repent, forgive them. Even if they sin against you seven times in a day and seven times come back to you saying I repent, you must forgive them." I have skeletons and classified secrets going to the grave with me, and I will rest in peace. I am not afraid and have the backbone to tell You that I have no regrets. My arrogance from payback was the sweetest revenge that allowed me to sleep better, knowing they were suffering without me even laying hands on them. Forgive me, Lord, because some bitterness still exists, and my forgiveness is still under construction. Approach with caution.

God, knowing that You are perfect is enough. Knowing that there is nobody like You is mind-blowing, and I will only answer to You. Amen.

Untitled #48

Dear God,

I have decided to live life to the fullest and dance while people watch. There is no shame in my game to stomp my feet and shake my hips as I please. However, I want people to see God's reflection by watching me as my arms are swaying in the sky in tune with the beat of my salvation. My rhythm and blues paint a clear picture of a perfect image of the genius who sculpted me from scratch out of the love He has for me. I am grateful to be considered one of His original masterpieces.

God has been good to me in ways I cannot explain. I have finally accepted that I deserve to be celebrated, appreciated, and loved on all levels of accomplishments, disappointments, and losses that may occur in my present or future. My current circumstances will never be considered my final destination, only death. So, until then, I will continue to dance.

I do not worry about which direction the wind is blowing because my crown is adjustable and shifts according to the momentum of the spirits of my guardian angels. (I am covered and protected in the name of Jesus). *Solid Truth and Testimonials* is just not about me speaking my truth or allowing strangers into an overly sensitive part of my private life and thoughts. It is me speaking the truth in admittance that I am not perfect. But as long as there is breath in my body, I'm willing to be a muse for the discouraged and unsure individuals stepping out on faith and taking risks worth every breath to reduce the stress levels of uncertainty in their bodies.

I have decided to live life to the fullest and dance while people watch. There is no shame in my game to stomp my feet and shake my hips as I please. However, I want people to see God's reflection when they see me while my arms are swaying in the sky in tune to the beat of my salvation. I want to snap my fingers to my rhythm and blues to paint a clear, realistic picture of the genius who sculpted me from scratch out of His love for me.

God has given me the audacity to be free and the freedom to be settled and comfortable in my skin. My new normal of self-love is dancing every time I get a chance, whether all eyes are on me or not. I realize that some people genuinely do not want to see me happy, and I am okay with that.

Turn up the music! Amen.

Untitled #49

Dear God,

Hebrew 11 says, "Now faith is confidence in what we hope for and assurance about what we do not see."

Thank You as always for allowing me to stretch my arms while yawning with stank breath and all this morning, knowing that You are restoring, blessing, and giving me the strength to plant my feet on solid ground again. Rise and shine, world! Whatever negativity, world, you have in store for me today, I rebuke it! Whatever roadblocks, world, you have created, I rebuke it! May the mercy and power of God create detours that get me over, straight through, or under the defeat because God says that I am bigger than my circumstances, and no weapons formed against me shall prosper.

Good morning, guardian angel of purpose. You know I have to greet you, too. This is another day we have to manifest positive energy and speak life to the impossible and disappoint the naysayers who do not vibe like us. All things are possible through Christ, who strengthens me.

Today, we are going to conquer all fears by being consistent and open to growth and opportunities that, with faith, will take us to the next level of success so that we can realize some childhood dreams and put to rest doubts and fears that do not exist. God promised in Psalm 37:4, "Take delight in the Lord, and He will give you the desires of your heart." Amen.

DEAR GOD,
IT'S STILL ME,
JANETTA

Untitled #50

Dear God,

I feel my faith is being tested because this devil has done everything to get me off course but no matter what obstacle may arise, failure is not an option. I will always push forward no matter what my circumstances may be. Consistency is the key, no matter how tired, discouraged, indecisive, and unmotivated I may become. This day, and every day, is the day You, God, have allowed, and I will be glad and rejoice in it. I feel like I am moving forward, standing still with a million thoughts and ideas bouncing around in my head with my feet still planted on solid ground. Instead of moving and acting while keeping my eyes on the prize and remaining positive that all things are possible through You, I am focusing on my circumstances, quietly being defeated and only feeling rejected because of my insecurities.

I want to give up, but my spirit won't allow me to bow down by giving the naysayers the satisfaction of seeing me out of character and as a failure. I never thought in a million years that I would write a book. But I did, and I am proud of myself. I never thought I would have been disciplined enough to set a goal as major as becoming an author. And the feeling of being published is amazing! I graduated from college when the odds were against me. The devil didn't like that I succeeded and managed a diversion by causing my alternator on my vehicle to go out. I couldn't be in attendance at my graduation ceremony, but that was okay. I finished with a 3.9 GPA, Cum Laude, respectfully from Florida A&M University. I am an alumnus.

God, I am changing and realizing my position as a queen, who has the impact to adjust crowns while possibly saving lives. I just get this feeling there is more significance to my life than scanning food and asking every other customer if they want paper or plastic for their groceries. I am supposed to be doing more, and I am constantly annoyed because I am not happy. I just can't settle for what is available, especially when I know the sky is the limit.

"Consider it pure joy, my brothers and sisters. Whenever you face trials of many kinds, because you know that the testing of our faith produces perseverance. Let perseverance finish it works so that you may be mature and complete, not lacking anything. If any of you lack wisdom, you should ask God, who gives generously without finding fault, and it will be given to you. But when you ask, you must believe and not doubt." James 1:2-6.

I am ready for success. I am ready to succeed, and I will be consistent. I will be encouraged by the word of God. Amen.

Untitled #51

Dear God,

You said in Philippians 4:6-7, "Do not be anxious about anything, but in every situation, by prayer and petition, with thanksgiving, present your requests to God. And the peace of God, which transcends all understanding, will guard your hearts and your minds in Christ Jesus."

I am trying my best to remain positive and focused because the devil is busy in all areas of my life, but trust me when I say that he will not win. The devil is trying to dim my light while I am standing center stage, confronting and dismissing old demons and new ones that I can no longer entertain or play Russian roulette. (This is a one-woman show). I am here, God, and I am giving all my lust, insecurities, brokenness, sadness, anything and everything that was orchestrated to destroy me, expose me, or even kill me to You. It is Your problem now. I can no longer complicate areas of this journey; the burden is getting too heavy for me to bear. I feel lost and defeated.

I am tired of getting up every morning at sunrise, second-guessing what I deserve, and questioning my next move. The world is unappreciative and unaccepting of the changes I have been through and still going through. But yet and still, I rise! Maya Angelou.

I have changed. It feels good to finally say it out loud and not feel frowned upon. I am here, God, standing center stage, starring in the biggest role of my life. Yet and still, the seats are empty, and no one is standing outside anxiously waiting to hear what I have to say.

However, my name is in bold print on the marquee: Janetta Lynne Jones. But yet and still, I am unrecognized.

I remain hopeful and patient, God, that someone is sitting out there watching, listening, and empathizing with my awful humble cry. It is not easy playing this role starring accountability, humbleness, forgiveness, and surrender.

Philippians 4:6-7, "Do not be anxious about anything, but in every situation, by prayer and petition, with thanksgiving, present your requests to God. And the peace of God, which transcends all understanding, will guard your hearts and your minds in Christ Jesus."

I am here, world, and I am ready. Please accept me and embrace me with open arms because I do not know how much time I have left. Amen.

Untitled #52

Dear God,

It's been a few days since I gave You my complete attention. I apologize for delaying what used to be daily conversations that have now turned into sessions by appointment only. (Or should I just say when I get the time). Making excuses about putting You last or in between is unacceptable. I have allowed the daily worldly living to interfere with someone who is my source and strength. (As weak as I am now, I should have kept You first). You always make the time for me, even while overseeing over a billion other souls daily; yet still, God, You think so fondly of me that You continue to support me through my foolishness and be there for me at times of need. I don't care what anybody else says; I still think I am Your favorite. Amen.

I love You, God, so much. I feel like I am not satisfied with my position as a queen. No matter how I keep readjusting this crown today, I can't accept the privileges because the responsibilities of being consistent and honorable are not standing in my favor today. No matter how trusting and understanding I try to be with others, loyalty has been disrespected at its finest. I am back to square one of being defensive, cold, short, and distant. I don't want to be angry anymore. I am over trying to find happiness in someone else, so what do I do, God? I am lying to my readers, and they need me for the truth because I can rest assured I am some of my readers' inspiration. I got to get back out of my way and lead by example. The people need me.

God, going days and sometimes weeks without our daily talks leaves me feeling lost and unsure. I don't like that feeling because I am nothing without You, and I am somebody with great confidence when I am with You. Not understanding the need of You and the importance of Your presence is dangerous especially to the individuals who are afraid to establish a relationship with You.

Hebrews 4:12-13, "For the word of God is alive and active. Sharper than any double-edged sword, it penetrates even to dividing soul and spirit, joints and marrow; it judges the thoughts and attitudes of the heart. Nothing in all creation is hidden from God's sight. Everything is uncovered and laid bare before the eyes of Him to whom we must give account."

Everything I do in secret from my heart, You openly reward, so the need to be loud and obnoxious is not necessary. I started a whole new journey without You, God. Some of the hiccups and not recognizing red flags or failing to acknowledge any issues got my head hurting, blood pressure semi-high, and the need to shut down is almost mandatory.

From this day forward, God, if it isn't sent by You, remove it!

If it's not going to mean me any good, remove it!

If it's not going to bring me peace, remove it!

If I ever allow anyone or any unnecessary circumstances to delay or cause any more interruptions in our friendship or daily worship with a humble soul and heavy heart, I want You to fix me, even if I am left with nothing, silence, and loneliness. I love You so much that after pouring my heart and putting my issues on the table about my shortcomings, I am still valid. My position as a queen is still relevant and accounted for. Amen.

BLACK MAN

Untitled #53

Dear God,

I will get up early in the morning and scramble my black man three eggs, seasoned with a little salt and pepper for taste, and whisk lightly. Slice up some veggies and then mix them with three kinds of cheese, reminding me of his kisses and how he switches up from my neck to my cheeks and then to the center of my lips. He is fresh like honeydew at room temperature in the summertime, although he is good and tasty all year round if you know what I mean. (Wink).

I accommodate those eggs with four slices of center-cut low sodium bacon (got to keep the blood pressure down and the feelings under control)—some French toast, heavy with the syrup, alongside a tab of butter. In conclusion, add a tall glass of fresh-squeezed naval orange juice to wash everything down. This man is everything; I will serve him hand and foot as the sunrises for a new day to begin. The hen is crowing, establishing my territory because he is my king.

I am coming in peace, waving my white flag with my right hand, and presenting my bruised heart with my left. Love is in the air and possible. I see the damage of life's defeats and the scars received from survival that life has left him on the edge but ready to surrender. It is time to live. It is time to laugh, and it is time to love. I am solid.

I understand the meaning of brokenness. I understand what it is like to lose complete control, trying to function in a judgmental and unforgiving world, especially when God has granted you His grace and mercy. You do not have to lick your wounds and prepare for the next battle. My love for you and our love for each other will end all wars and heal all wounds. My love is sufficient. Good morning. Amen.

Untitled #54

Dear God,

Sometimes he is too good to be true. But in all actuality, he is good, and he is my truth. He is the secret ingredient to my happiness and the shift to new behaviors dealing with self-control, trust, communication, and love. He is my dream come true and someone worth letting my guard down and allowing him the honor to loving someone broken, yet guarded, like me.

Psalms 37:4 says, "Take delight in the Lord, and He will give you the desires of your heart." He and I found each other at a time in our lives when healing, forgiveness, and trust were nonexistent, and happiness was only meant for certain individuals but not for the broken, real, and rebellious ones, like us. I describe us as savages because we were so free, cutthroat, and unapologetic about our business. We were free in worldly behaviors, not caring about the cause and effects of others and our actions. (Karma has served us both, and our behaviors have been corrected).

Happiness is a major factor in our lives now because too much time has already been wasted, but fate has been preparing us to be peaceful and decent human beings for each other. Life has served us enough bull; it's time to flip the script. Nobody is auditioning for brokenhearted and player roles anymore, and it is time for longevity and commitment. (I do if it ever comes down to it).

It is time to heal and experience ecstasy in a way that has never been smoked, swallowed, or inhaled before. (This is a natural high). It is time for good stuff and real stuff that can be built because our

43

foundation was established by mutual understanding and open conversations about his definition of loyalty and my definition of being solid. (Same thing but different perspectives).

Enough bridges from ex-lovers have been burned from past insignificant others. Too much time and too many tears have been cried to keep reflecting and revisiting old scripts that have already been seen and heard.

Sometimes, I feel like he is too good to be true. But in all actuality, he is good, and he is my truth. He is the secret ingredient to my now happiness and new behaviors dealing with self-control, trust, communication, and love. He is somebody worth loving, and the man, if God allows, worth me spending the rest of my life with because he is now mixed in my dish. And the secret of happiness is ready to be served. Amen.

Untitled #55

Dear God,

I do not even know how to feel right now because You are allowing me to spread my wings in a way I never imagined possible. I want to start by saying, Thank You! You know I have trust issues, Lord, and You know I am admitting naivety when it comes to men and love; however, because I am not able to distinguish who is solid and worthy to be a part of my succession, I stand still and wait for You to speak to my heart. I want to make sure I hear You loud and clear. No more being brokenhearted.

God, I am glad that You are restoring everything I lost and rebuilding everything that has crumbled through loneliness and desperation. I cut loose my Pinocchio's and have devoted my time to a man who is worth loving and giving my complete undivided attention to. I call him heaven sent. Psalm 147:3, "He heals the brokenhearted and binds up their wounds."

The security of being vulnerable and the reassurance that my emotions and heart are in a safe place has allowed me to lower my weapons of being guarded and look ahead. For once in my life, I believe love is possible.

Speak to my heart, God. I am listening and ready to open up to him in ways I never imagined before. You are allowing me to spread my wings, and the breeze of the wind is soothing and ruffling my feathers; that is comforting to my heart and soul. I am ready to fly.

I have a man in my life who inspires me and is consistently proving that I am needed and recognizing that I am a queen. Halleluiah! He is worth building an empire for; our foundation will be grounded with love brick by brick. So, no matter how rough the earth may quake or ache, we will be solid.

God, before I take a leap of faith and risk hitting the cement that formulated these broken pieces of hardships, unworthiness, lack of trust from family and old lovers, this material must be tried on the beauty of Your word.

Ephesians 3:17-19, "...so that Christ may dwell in your hearts through faith. And I pray that you, being rooted and established in love, may have power, together with the Lord's holy people, to grasp how wide and long and high and deep is the love of Christ, and to know this love that surpasses knowledge—that you may be filled to the measure of all the fulness of God." I am, or should I say, we are ready for war.

God, I understand his wounds and the heartaches from a world that is so judgmental and does not give two shakes about sacrifice and the necessary steps, decisions, and the pressure of keeping our heads above the water for survival.

It is a shame that he and I have existed all this time in this world without each other until now. Amen.

Untitled #56

Dear God,

I don't expect everybody to understand our relationship and what I discuss with You, and honestly, it's none of their business. However, I think it is reasonable to share the nature of our relationship and how comfortable I am discussing my issues and random thoughts with You. That's just the best kind of friend of mine that You are; well, at least to me.

God, I have the greatest secret I want to tell the whole wide world, but I am afraid. People's opinions can be so judgmental and cruel, and I don't want outside opinions to contaminate this newfound pleasure. This conversation is open, and I have to get this off my chest. You did something unimaginable that I haven't had the chance to process, even though it is happening before my eyes as I write.

I have someone in my life that You perfectly aligned me with, and he compliments my spiritual growth and independence to be free in a world constantly finding me guilty of surrendering my truth. You have allowed me to let my guard down in a way I said I would never do. You have created a space in my heart for peace and reconciliation because I deserve to be happy. When I look into my king's eyes, I see he deserves happiness, too. I have a secret treasure I will keep forever off-limits from pirates and sacred for historians to discover when we are dead and gone—our legacy of love.

Yes, God, he and I are going down in history as the best love story ever written from being broken to fixed in Your name and unstoppable because the secret was well kept and ordained in Your great timing. A king and queen were established in a season of abundance, overflowing with new beginnings, entangled with a pinch of paradise, and raw crystal-clear truth of past disappoints that can no longer contaminate or expose false accusations of our legacy. We are healing.

I am going to love this man; I am going to allow him to love me, too. We are healing.

God, I have the best secret in the world, and I wish I could stand at the top of somebody's mountaintop and scream to the top of my lungs and listen to my echo bounce off the mountain walls and return to my ears. I am assured that my truth comes back, instead of bouncing further into the open world, because my secret of being in love with this king should be safe and protected with me.

Yes, God, he and I are going down in history as the best love story ever written from being broken to fixed in Your name and unstoppable because the secret was well kept and ordained in Your timing. He and I were established in a season of abundance with the overflow of raw crystal-clear truths of past disappoints that can no longer contaminate us, break us, separate us, or make false accusations of our newfound positions as king and queen. We are healing.

We will be in love, and this conversation between You and I will be the best-kept secret I have never told out loud. Amen.

Untitled #57

Dear God,

The devil is busy trying to kill my spirit and trying his best to destroy everything I have worked hard to replenish and protect for safekeeping. My sanity is of value; I must stay balanced and in control, no matter how heavy the burden. My daughter is of value; I have to set the example and lead unafraid and unapologetic because there is no room for weakness. I am risking it all by denying flesh for spiritual maturity and growth so I can rest in peace in eternity in heaven with my Savior Jesus Christ when the time comes. My legacy will live on in the hearts of those I have touched and loved. My name will remain relevant, published on bookshelves across the world.

The devil is causing chaos in my life by starting flames of confusion just when I was coming to a breakthrough of finally being able to see the sun at the break of dawn after years of trying to tame uncontrollable wildfires. The devil is so busy that he is restarting the healing process from scratch and bringing attention to my eyes and heart that I thought were aligned to heal. However, it is still defiant and in mourning of life, and past disappointments and old wounds are reopening while forgiveness goes back to step one of the grieving process.

The stitches have been ripped, and the devil is having his way, making me cry and wish I had never allowed him that close or even allowed him comfort to beat me down the way he tends to do. I am in denial about my right now, and God's will for my future. So the best thing I can do is stand still and pray harder with my face in the palm of my hands.

I refuse to believe I am prospering no matter how many checks or lines have been crossed through from the bucket list of things to accomplish. I am sometimes in denial about the truth and question if there is light at the end of the tunnel, especially when it feels like I am continuously feeling my way through and developing calluses on the palms of my hands. I am tired of fighting, but I am keeping my head above the water. I do not know how to swim, and I refuse to panic or reactivate my adrenaline.

The devil is busy, but that is okay. My truth has been solidified. I am here to say that as long as I can breathe while floating on my back while the water is immerging over my body, I know I will simply be fine. I am in denial that I have forgiven myself because every day, when I try to acknowledge my growth and strength, the black man is starting to beat me down with his arrogance and mean ole backbone.

The devil is busy. Amen.

Untitled #58

Dear God,

I give black man too much power to play around with my emotions, especially when I am putting everything on the line, like being vulnerable, available, and exclusive. I give him my undivided attention by serenading him with my love language, something so powerful that everybody is scared of confronting. But I am not, and that is my truth.

I am bold and have the audacity to admit that for him. I am willing to put my heart on the line by risking it all for love and the sake of happiness. I am willing to step out on faith for a feeling I have no earthly idea about. But happiness is a pleasure that is much needed between my legs and in my spiritual growth, and that is me solidifying my truth because I am trying to survive. I am too real for these niggas.

I need a man who is not afraid to be free and willing to put in the time to maintain a mending heart and misguided soul. I need a consistent man saying what he means and meaning what he says because I need to be held accountable for my disposition as his woman, especially when he officially crowns me as his queen. I will be his backbone, balancing the weight by having my shoulders there to hold him up if he stumbles and my chest out so that he can rest because this life does get hectic. My king will always have my back available; he needs somebody to lean on. If I were his woman, I would hold him accountable for his actions of consistency. I have to have order and be properly tamed to be supportive and grounded.

I will hold him accountable because this woman has been lost and scorned from the world beating her down with imperfections and unhealthy relationships controlled by lack of security. I am tired of blaming the past for my downfalls or using bad relationships as an excuse for not healing. Being broken and staying broken is a choice, and being fixed is a decision.

I have given him too much power to play around with my emotions, and it's starting to make me cry. He keeps hurting my feelings because of his lack of consistency and communication, calling foul by throwing the ball back in my court. The power I allowed this man sends shockwaves like an earthquake through my veins, making me stand still to recognize how he is abusing the authority I am giving him to consider loving me. Amen.

Untitled #59

Dear God,

Today, I didn't know whether I was coming or going; the distractions of my anxiety had the best of me. I was polluting, causing turnarounds and avoidance in the aisles because of my insecurity issues with my black man. I lay in bed, replaying our old and new conversations, trying to understand why we are so unbalanced, bickering like two children going back and forth, talking about who hit who first. The honeymoon phase is over; it's time to bring all our tools, the blueprint, and the essentials to keep us solid and hopefully together since I was hoping for longevity. My self-regard is fighting to keep us grounded. (Talk about being considerate). But this pill has been tough to swallow because he is hardheaded, on self-defense, and on guard from his present and past issues.

Instead of leaning on You, God, for understanding, I was leaning on my understanding of Proverbs 5-6, "Trust in the Lord with all your heart and lean not on your own understanding; in all your ways submit to him, and he will make your paths straight." Please, God, settle my stomach and allow me to make my decisions based on what is good for my daughter and me, not on unrealistic expectations that are not in alignment with what You have for my life.

I have been thinking about cheating on this man. I have even thought about returning to old ways and habits. I thought I could indulge in him and not juggle strings of Pinocchio's who would rather watch their nose grow instead of being real men. I think I am too real, and I am emotionally unavailable. I am tired of my black man and his bull crap! (Excuse my language).

God, I am searching for peace and clarity. I need to end this feeling of uncertainty and come to a conclusion about this love because I am mentally and emotionally disturbed. Forgive my language, but You said that I am allowed to express myself and be open and vulnerable in our relationship, God. Amen.

Untitled #60

Dear God,

Today is October 19, and the last time we spoke was October 10, literally on paper. But in all actuality, God, I have been connecting with You in my thoughts, having indirect conversations of false perceptions of my reality, goals, and hopeful accomplishments. I refuse to accept that all final decisions are required to align with Your will for my life instead of what I feel is best for me. The solid truth is that You know what's best for me, and I am taking risks anyway by putting up with unnecessary distractions. I have realized, yet again, that I am nothing without You and somebody when I am living for You—what a wonderful feeling.

Today, God, I decided I would not argue or allow anyone or anything to steal my joy or to disturb my peace. Today, God, I decided to surrender all and move freely and in peace with my white flag and Jesus' piece across my heart while my lips are muttering Psalm 27, "The Lord is my light and salvation, whom shall I fear?" Making no excuses and giving no power to anyone or anything to steal the joy; I am stirring up from the pit of my gut to mix well with happiness, overshadow the doubt and fears of the unknown, and outshine anyone trying to seek, kill, or destroy this digestion of self-gratitude. I will rise to the occasion. "When the wicked advance against me to devour me, it is my enemies and my foes who will stumble and fall. Though any army besiege me, my heart will not fear; though war break out against me, even then I will be confident." Psalm 27.

Giving my life to You, God, was the best thing I have ever done. Loving You is like repeatedly listening to Nina Simone on a cool summer day, feeling good and knowing that You know how I feel. I feel good.

God, I live my life on the edge, facing the unknown of tomorrow and the demands of today by expecting to get through life's obstacles, not making any excuses because all things are possible through Christ. I am in acceptance of Your will to be done and not mine. Everything You align for my future is golden and, of course, solid. My stubborn inhumane ways will never again have me turn a deaf ear to You. Amen.

Untitled #61

Dear God,

My heart is broken. By allowing myself to be free and naïve in love/lust, I allowed this black man to let me down in a way I thought was impossible. I was hoping the foundation we supposedly created was built on trust, truth, and understanding; was solid and untouched like the love You have for me, God. John 4 17:8, "God is love, who-ever lives in love lives in God, and God in them. This is how love is made complete among us so that we will have confidence on the day of judgment: In this world we are like Jesus. There is no fear in love. But perfect love drives out fear, because fear has to do with punish-ment. The one who fears is not made perfect in love."

I haven't been healing; the road to recovery has been distracted by the butterflies in my stomach. Love is slowly deteriorating. All the courage I have built to speak my truth and the manifestations of self-love I exemplified feels like it has fallen apart. I am back to giving the black man the power to make me feel less, unwanted, and unap-preciated when I know deep down in my gut that I am adequate. I am empty, still unraveling, trying to fit the description of being enough in my black man's eyes and not enough in Your eyes, God, and in mine. Like Toni Braxton said, "Here goes another sad love song, racking my brain like crazy, and I am all torn up."

I am losing control; I no longer feel safe or secure in this relation-ship. He acts as if my loss of interest doesn't faze him. My black man does not have the desire he once had for me. The betrayal is in his messages I discovered of him reaching out to other women with hidden fantasies and conversations that had nothing to do with me, which breaks my heart and hurts my feelings. I feel let down.

My heart is broken, God. I am uncomfortable and in shambles of what the next move should be. I am resting next to a man I no longer recognize; I am recognizing the repetitive cycle of another failed love. But this time, I understand the assignment. I get the season we are in.

He was a lesson, and I stood my ground with no regrets. Amen.

Untitled #62

Dear God,

Loving my black man is not easy. Every day, I try to adjust to his attitude and behaviors by catering to his wants, setting aside my personal needs, which are feeling secure as his queen in this relationship, being confident in my skin while being assertive, and an important aspect in his life. But it's draining me because I am putting his needs before my own, and I am tired. I am no longer adjustable.

My black man and I are both damaged from childhood misconceptions of what healthy relationships are supposed to look like. It's hard for us to imitate what we in our heads perceive love to be when we both have mommy and daddy issues. I failed him miserably. Instead of being my authentic self, I started arguments and pushed unnecessary buttons, trying to control how I wanted him to love me by creating the narrative of how I felt he should love me instead of just letting him love according to his perception. We are not like the Huxtables from *The Cosby Show* or the Smiths from *The Fresh Prince of Bel-Air*. Love is not as easy as some couples make it look, but I find it easier living without him than with him. (I need my peace, and stability is important).

My black man is like no other; he is far from Prince Charming as written and described from some once upon a time fairytale. He didn't come onto the scene on a horse with a sword; he showed up as a single father with two little girls, three and five years old. My black man showed up with the expectancy of me being phenomenal, which I am. But the only problem is, I am not that phenomenal woman for him.

I am no longer emotionally available to his needs or thoughts. I am mentally drained from nonnegotiable arguments. I am resetting boundaries that should have never been crossed in the first place. I am not physically satisfied, and I will no longer beg or ask for what I know I deserve from this black man. Amen.

Untitled #63

Dear God,

Am I reliving old mistakes with my black man? What am I doing? Why is he here? Most importantly, why did I allow him to come back? I am not happy! Why am I afraid to let go? I am emotionally unavailable and upset with him and myself. He does not feed me spiritually, nor do I feel like he is enough to lead me or be an example of a father figure for my child. His loyalties are being compromised by his selfish wants and not focusing on what this family needs, what this queen needs, and the structure of a stable foundation for his own children's needs because of his hidden motives and desires. God, I am making excuses and creating false realities again, thinking I can change him, and I can't. I am so frustrated that I am venting. I have to refer to *Solid Truths and Testimonials: Volume 1* because I need to encourage myself with my own words.

I will not care. I will not care, and I will stay in control! I will stay in control. I will stay in control. I will stay in control. I will stay in control. I will stay in control. I will stay in control.

Get out of my feelings. Get out of my feelings. Get out of my feelings. Get out of my feelings.

I deserve better. I deserve better. I deserve better. I deserve better. I deserve better. I deserve better. I deserve better. I deserve better. I deserve better. I deserve better. I deserve better. I deserve better. I deserve better. I deserve better. I do deserve better!

I will not tolerate disrespect. I will not tolerate disrespect. I will not tolerate disrespect. I will not tolerate disrespect. I will not tolerate disrespect.

I am good on my own. I am good on my own. I am good on my own. I will be good on my own. (In tears). Amen.

LESSON
LEARNED

Untitled #64

Dear God,

I stood up for myself. This time around, I didn't make any excuses or try to justify the exiting of my now ex-black man from my life. I am trying my best not to entertain negative thoughts of our breakup. My intentions for him and his children were good; my objective was to graduate from being a girlfriend to fiancé and then possibly his wife. I had it all visualized and planned out in my head as one big happy family because that has been one of my heart's desires ever since I was a little girl.

I wanted to mother his children. They needed a queen to look up to, and I was prepared to nurture an additional two because they needed guidance. I was willing to make myself available for them and treat them as if they were my own, even when their behaviors were disrespectful, defiant, and difficult. I tried to remain calm and patient. But as time went on, the task was causing me to turn a deaf ear to my biological child. She was suffering in silence because they were so needy for attention and constantly had to be redirected and disciplined. I wasn't paying attention to her loneliness, and she suffered in silence. Yet, she was still loving and patient despite my insubordination to her needs.

I can admit, God, that I was excited in the beginning. In my heart, I thought I had hit the lottery of love because he appeared to be everything I wanted and asked for. Periodically, I had to refer to my checklist to make sure he wasn't too good to be true. (But I forgot the devil could make things and people look good, too). I thought I had a family so well blended that I didn't have to conceive because he already had two little girls of his own and three was the number of completion for me. Between You, God, and me, I was hoping to lowkey have a baby boy. Anyway, that was just my selfish desire.

Now that I am alone in my house and it is silent, I can finally hear Your voice without the yelling and screaming. My mind is at peace with the acceptance of being single and sleeping in a queen size bed alone, now able to keep rolling over without him in the way. I don't know if he was a test, God. But I stood my ground, even when he was being manipulative, orchestrating his hidden motives, trying to make me think I was weak-minded, and had me questioning my values. He almost had me reorganizing my goals and questioning my future when I had this dream of becoming great and being great before he even came into the picture. This black man had me on the edge. Even in my uncertainty, all he had to do was make good love to me so that my flesh was willing to settle for whatever lies and false realities he created to mess with my brain.

Black man knew what to do to calm me down and make me think our relationship wasn't as bad as it was. But my heart knew better, and when the light bulb finally clicked on and stayed on, I knew he was more of a liability than an asset, which left me with no choice but to let him and those children go. (My daughter comes first, and this situation was a lesson well learned).

The thought of this black man lying beside me made me feel a little relief. Finally, for a moment, I didn't have to juggle so many hats of being the teacher, preacher, accountant, nurse, and doctor because he allowed me to have a break and balanced things out. I was tired of carrying what felt like the whole world on my shoulders. My ex-black man was what I needed in that season, a provider and a protector, and I can admit I felt safe. We had a great time laughing and being underneath each other; it was comfortable and something new for us.

I know for sure, God, that You don't play about me, and You don't play about Your children. You said that the weapons would form, but they wouldn't prosper. You heard conversations and saw things hidden from me that he was doing behind my back. You protected my daughter and me, and I am so forever grateful. I have been solid since the beginning of this relationship. The funny thing is, I went from cooking this black man breakfast every morning to packing and carrying his belongings out the door and loading them into his truck before dinnertime. Good night.

The reason was to recognize my value, stand on my boundaries, and let go unapologetically. The lesson learned: Just because a man is good to me doesn't mean that he is the one for me. (Adjusted crown). Amen.

OUTRO

Untitled #65

Dear Birth Mother,

I just want to start this one-sided conversation by saying that I love you. I am not upset with you, now that I am mature and in my adult life, for putting me up for adoption, not knowing if keeping me was an option or not. You did what you had to do; I cannot fault you for that, so relax. (I did not come to tear you down, so let your defenses down. I come in peace). I do not know you. But I miss you, and I hope that someday if God allows, we can reconnect and get an understanding of each other. I was hoping that maybe you would be able to explain why we could not be together. The only link I ever had with you was when I was inside you while carrying me in your belly.

I wish I knew what it was like to be held by you. I wish I knew what it was like to know if you looked at me with love or were you disgusted after birthing me. Nobody but the doctors and whoever else was in that delivery room at the Hollywood Memorial knows the truth from forty-one years ago.

Did you fight for me, or did you give up on me? Please, think wisely and be honest with your response because I will listen carefully and look deep into your eyes, analyzing and searching for truth. I missed a woman I never knew and could not even describe or pick out in a police lineup if forced to, even if it was to save my life.

Did you talk to me, or did you turn a deaf ear to my newborn cry? Was it hard, or was it easy to say goodbye, knowing that you would never see me again? Did you ever think about me or wonder if I was all right? After all these years of living in the unknown and living without me, do I even matter to you? You still matter to me, and I am always thinking of you.

Birth mother, I have been missing you. I feel the emotions we have in common, and I can relate to you in weakness, strength, and perseverance. I lost babies because of stress and abuse but was saved by one, and disconnecting myself from her would be impossible. She saved me from myself. I was reborn and gave my life to Christ. I could not imagine signing my rights away, even if it were for my best interest, because of any lack of stability or foundation. But I am not judging you because our situations were different.

I am in the process of trying to heal. I have been hurt for an exceptionally long time. If I can reconnect with the root, then maybe I can get some relief, or maybe the process can finally begin. Every day, I start over from scratch.

I remember when the abuser used to beat me down after having bad days. I used to sit by my window, crying my little heart out, hoping and wishing you could hear my cry, but you never did. I even tied sheets together to naively think I could connect it to my pigtails to let my hair down like Rapunzel, and you would climb up to save me, but you never did.

In conclusion, birth mother, my truth has been solidified. I am silent for now. I wish you would have kept me. I would not have minded facing life storms with you. My life has not been terrible, but it has been a constant battle to fit in and be accepted because of negligence of understanding where I come from. I have a baby girl who keeps me updated and strong, and I understand the word sacrifice because I am a mom. I appreciate you sacrificing me, even if it meant saving your life. In a weird way, you saved mine, too, and I will always love you for that.

About the Author

Janetta Lynne Jones is a poet and author of her second published book titled, *Solid Truths and Testimonials: Volume 2, Dear God.* Janetta has a bachelor's degree in criminal justice from Florida Agricultural Mechanical University, which she received on August 3, 2013.

A long-time resident of Tallahassee, Florida, Janetta has been writing poetry and short stories since she was in the ninth grade at Lincoln High School. Janetta has one daughter whom she loves dearly and hopes she will learn lessons, find self-discovery, and understand the struggles and sacrifices her mother has made to become the woman she is today.

Facebook: Janetta Lynne Jones

Instagram: @strong_and_black

Email: Solidtruthsandtestimonials@yahoo.com

About the Cover Artist

Kenya Henry, Jr., is also known as the artist Kenya Wolf. Art and design were not his career paths of choice, but he decided to take an art class in his senior year of high school, took it seriously, and found out that art was his hidden talent.

"Even though I figured out my purpose in life, there's a moral to this story for everyone. Step out of your comfort zone and give 110 percent every time. You never know what doors you can open."

Instagram: @whoiskenyawolf

Facebook: Kenya Wolf

Thank you for reading my second book of solid truths and testimonials. See you next time.

Made in United States
Orlando, FL
29 April 2022